Sultry Indian Erotica

exotic adult coloring

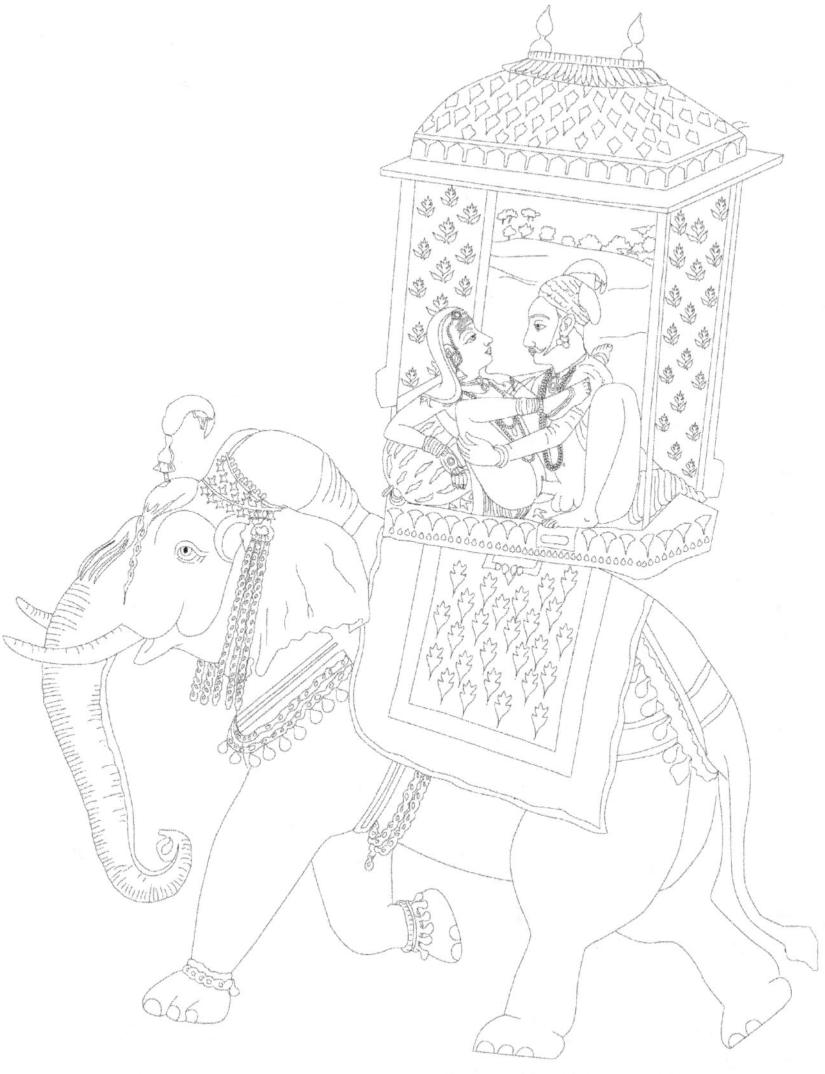

by natalie tate

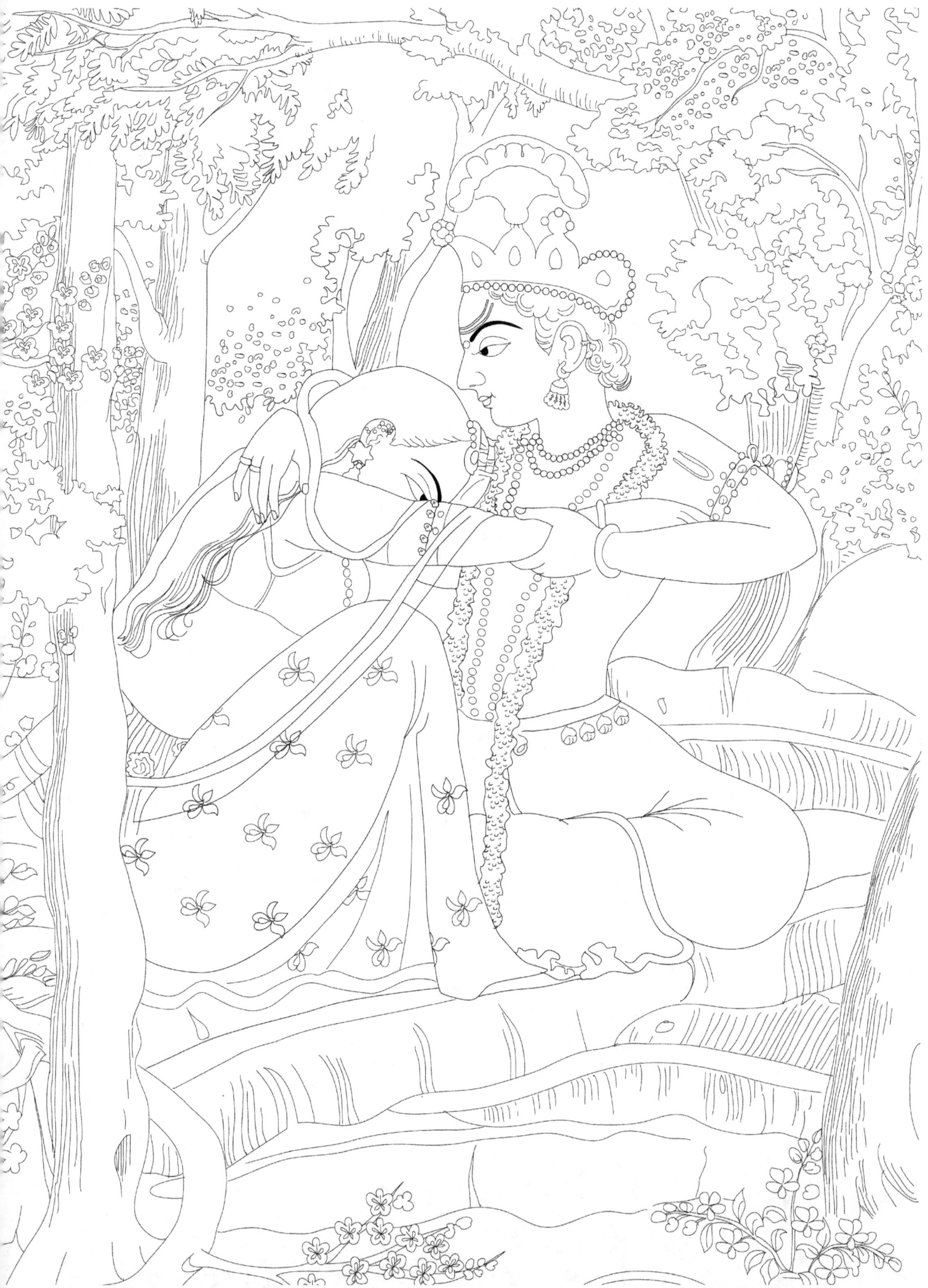

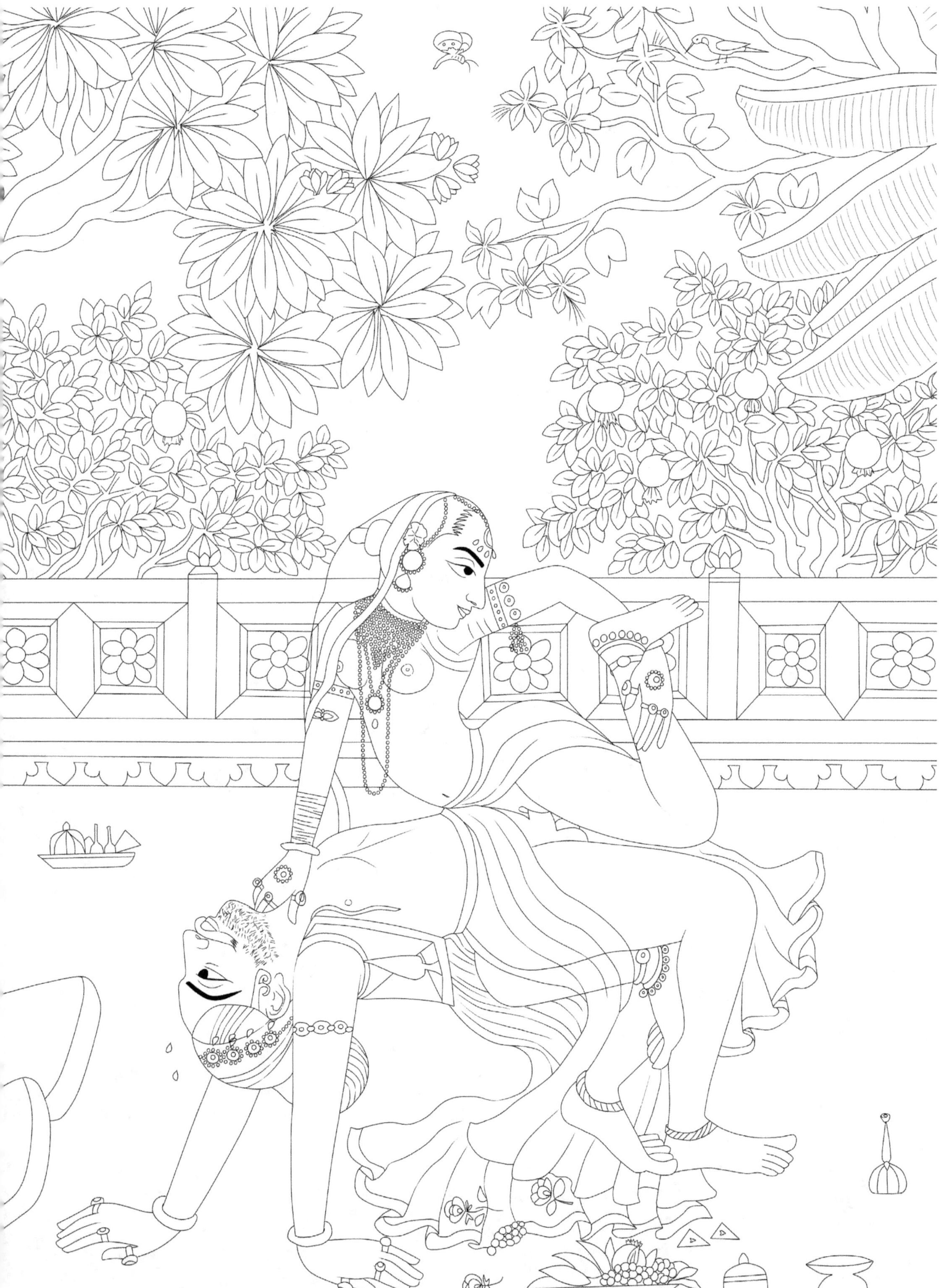

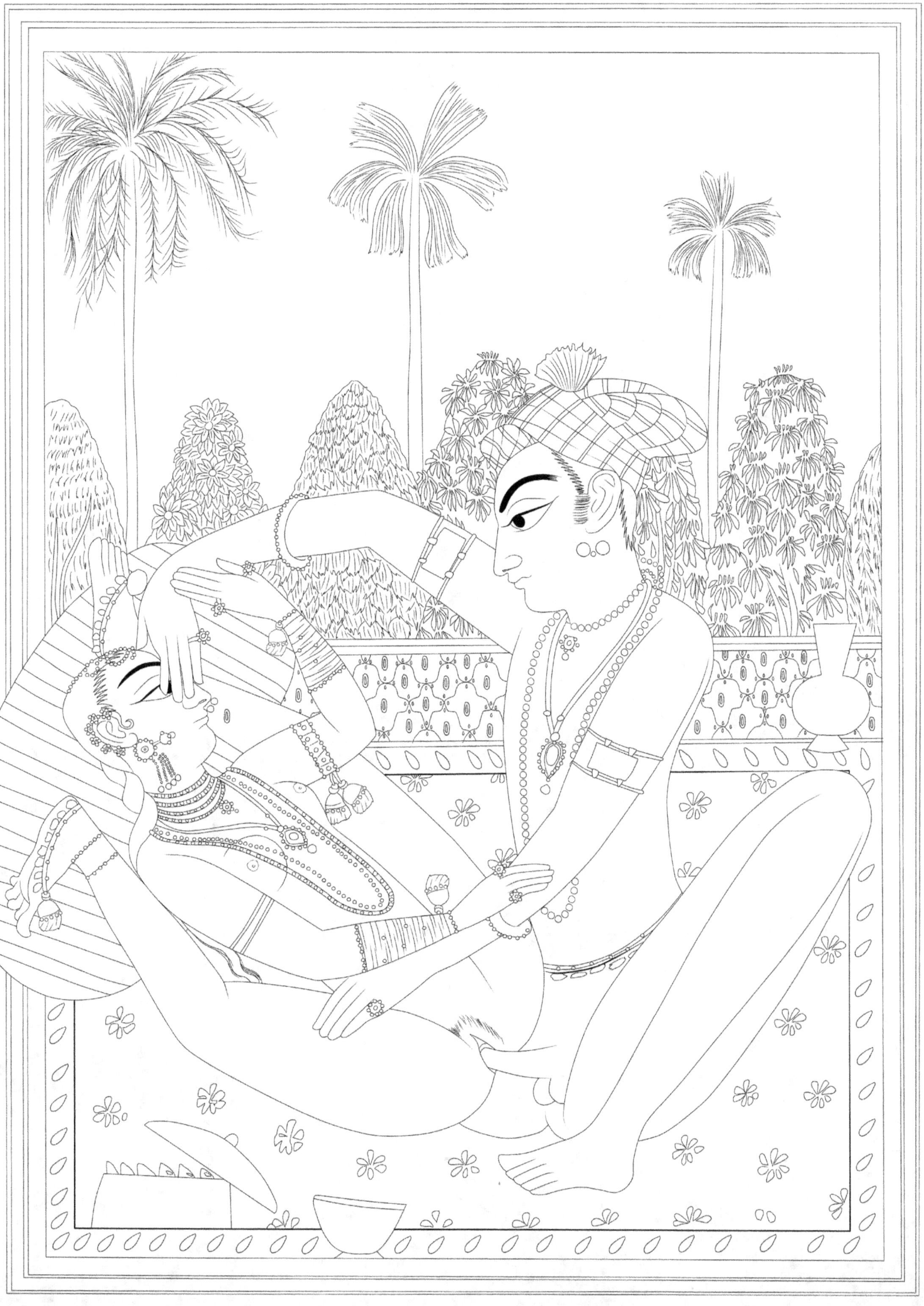

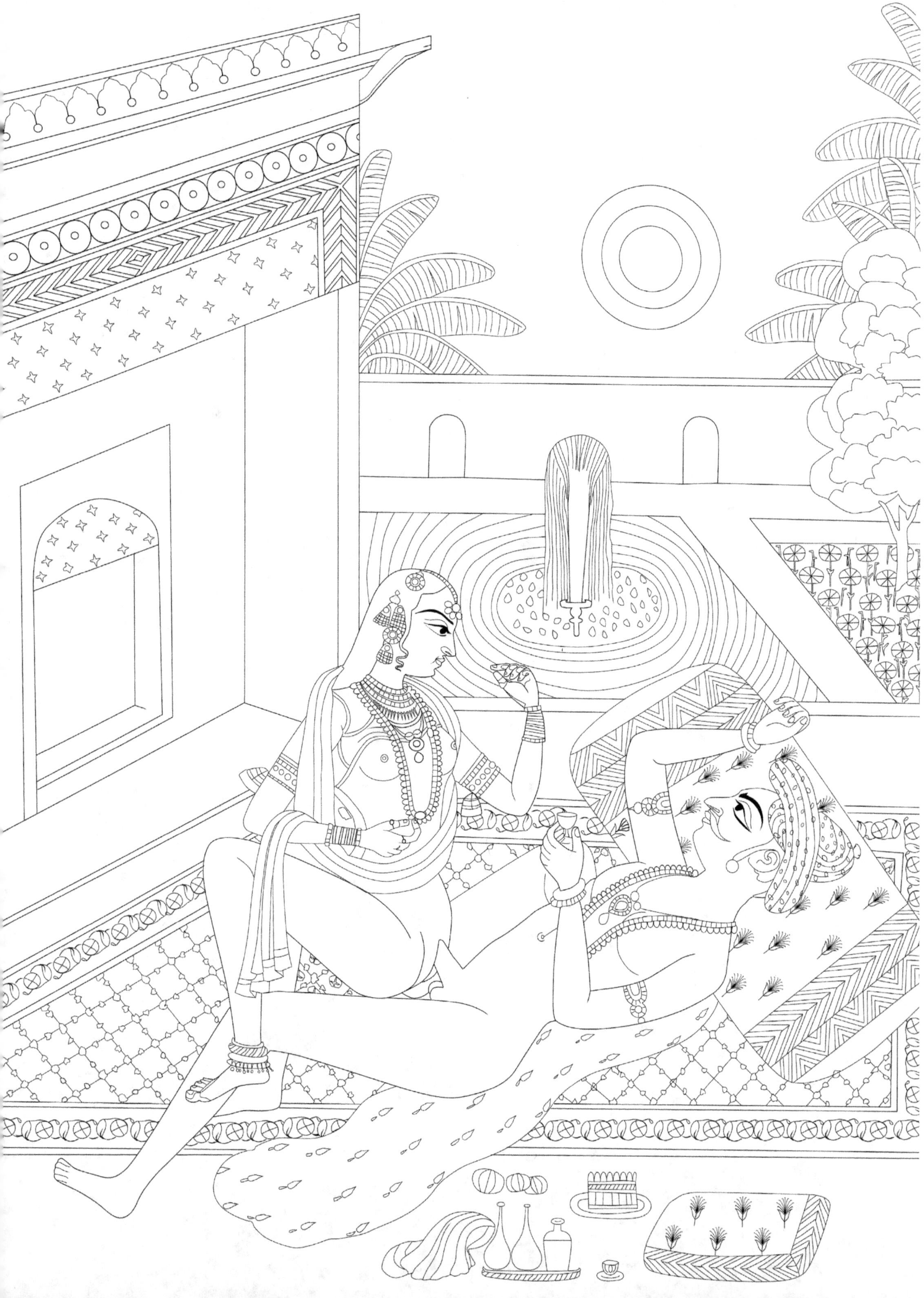

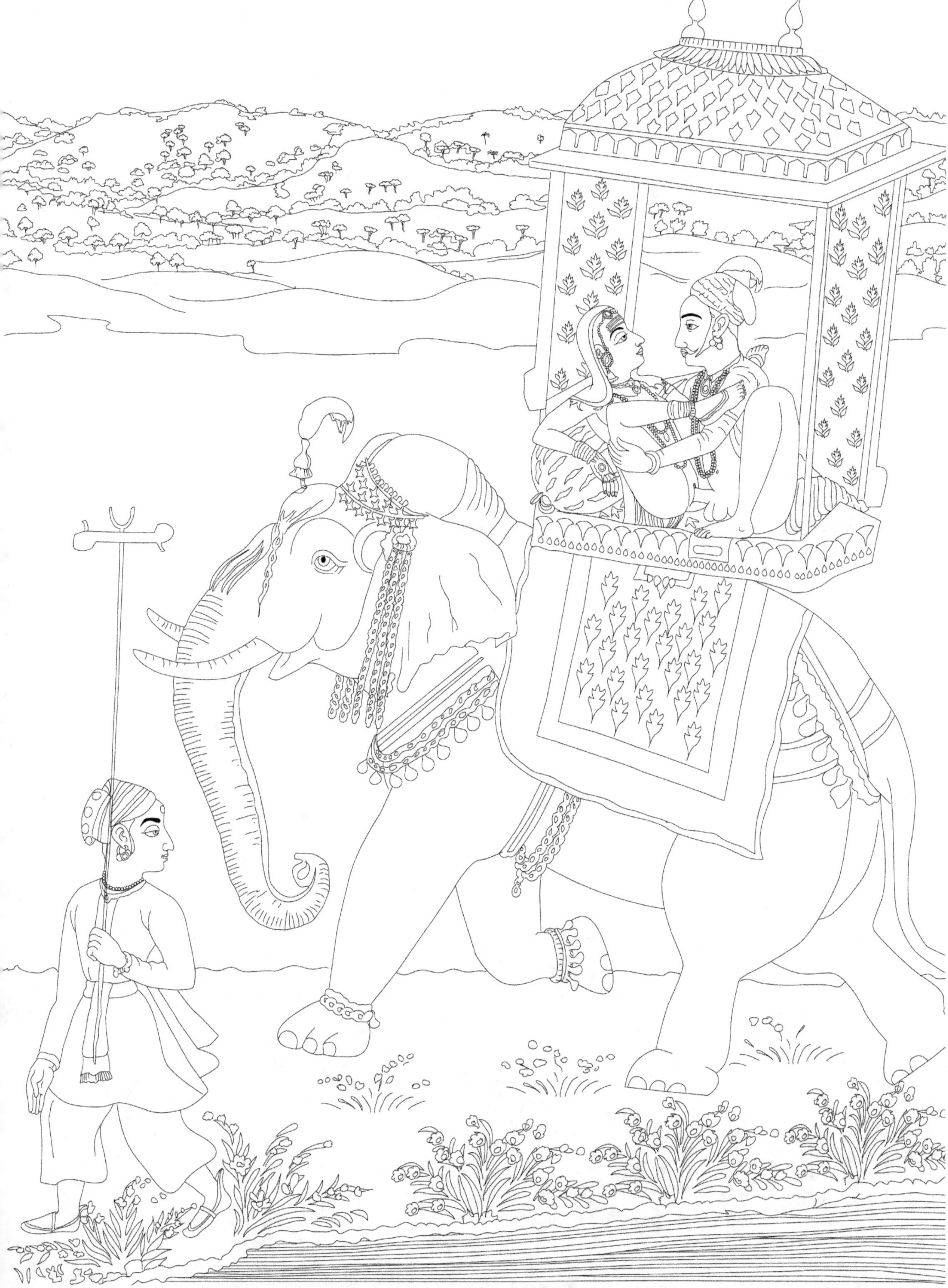

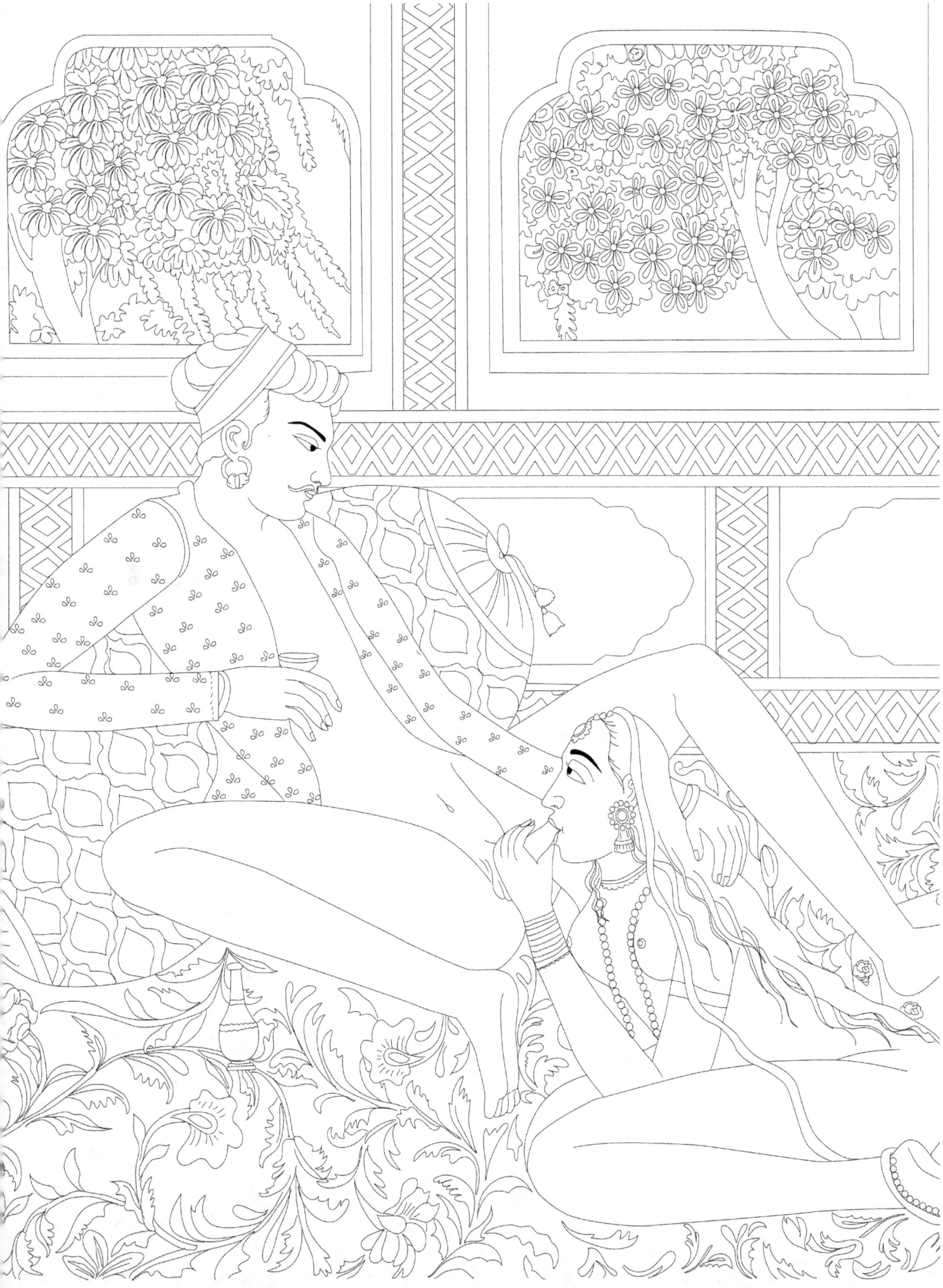

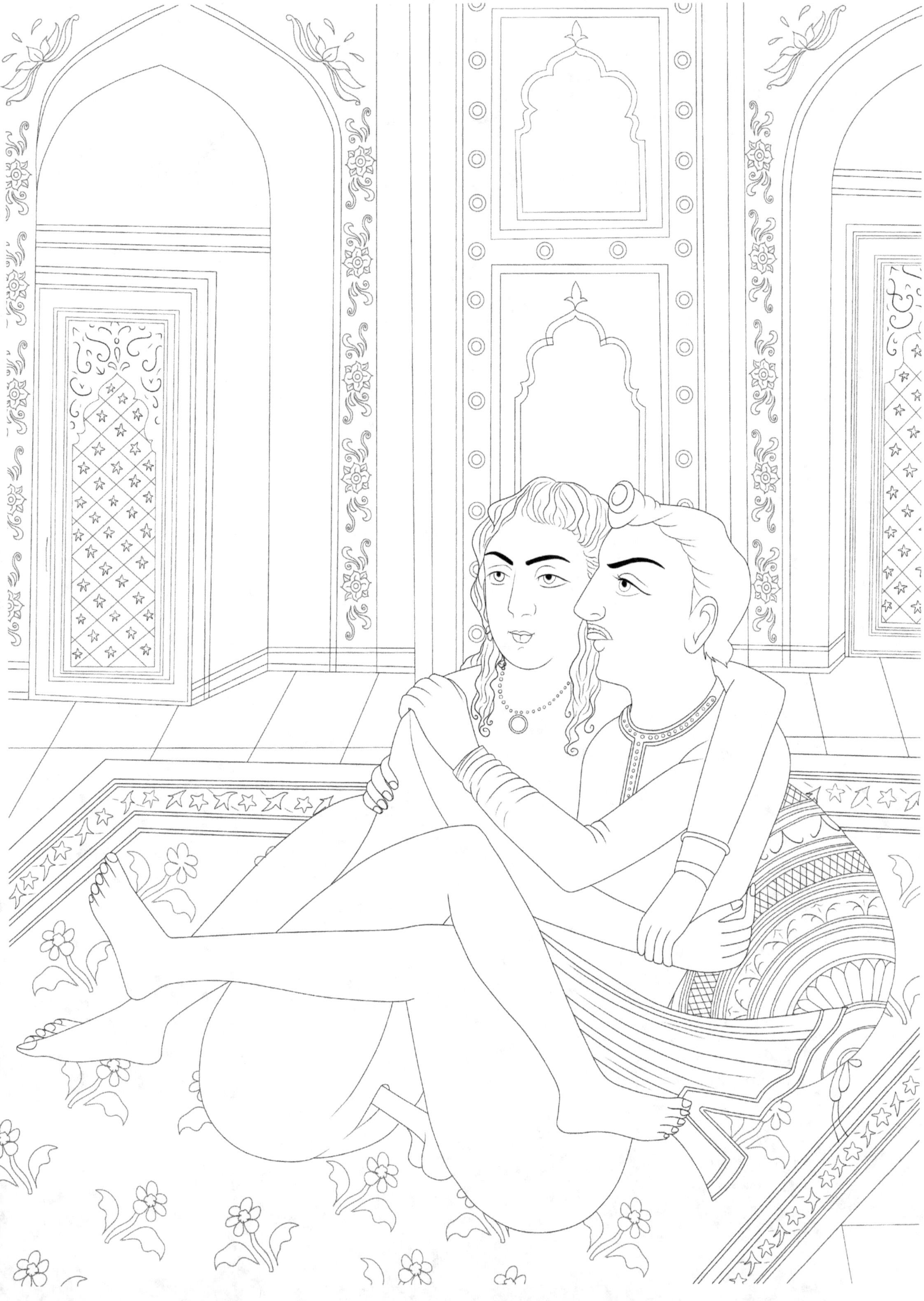

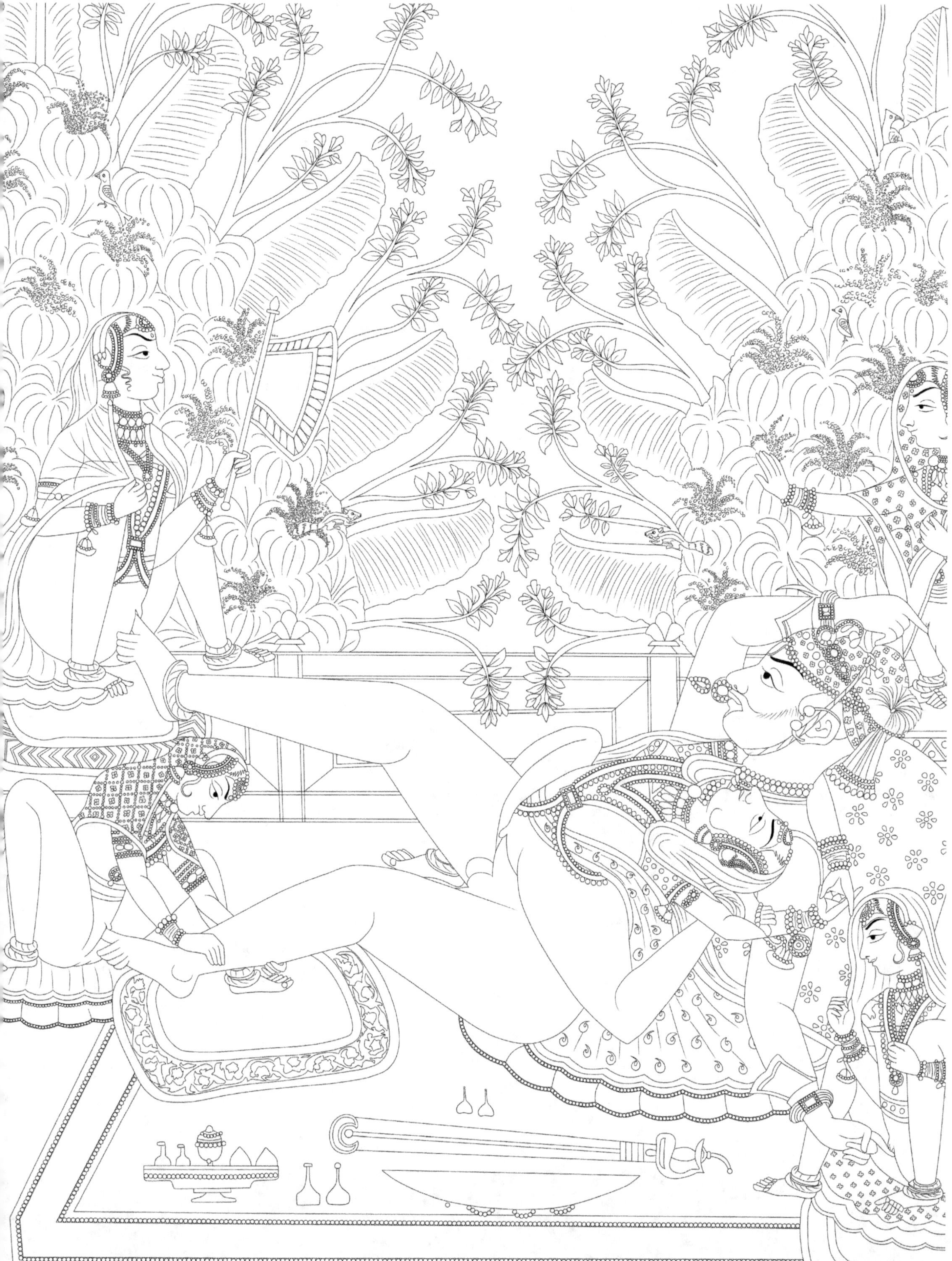

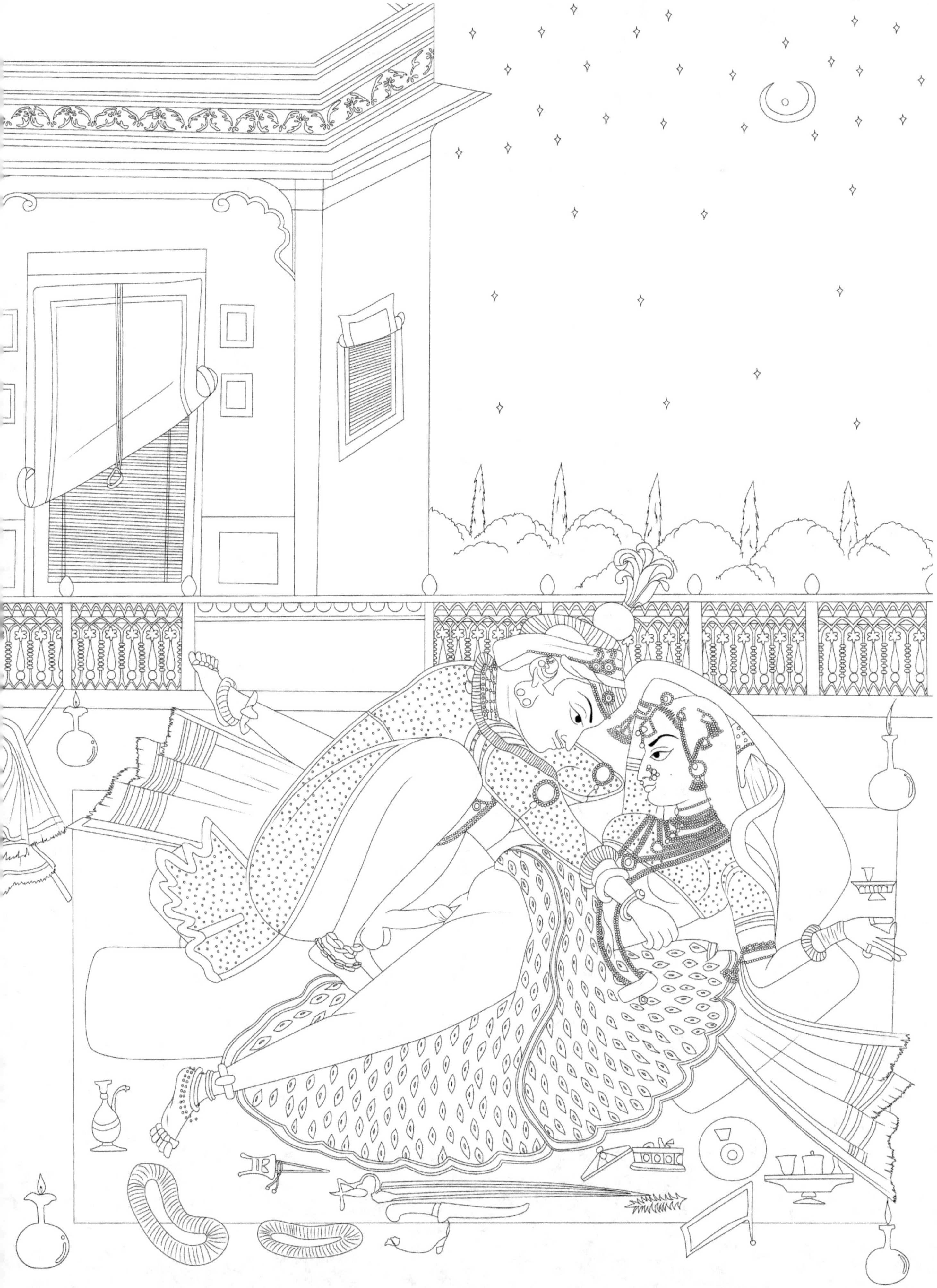

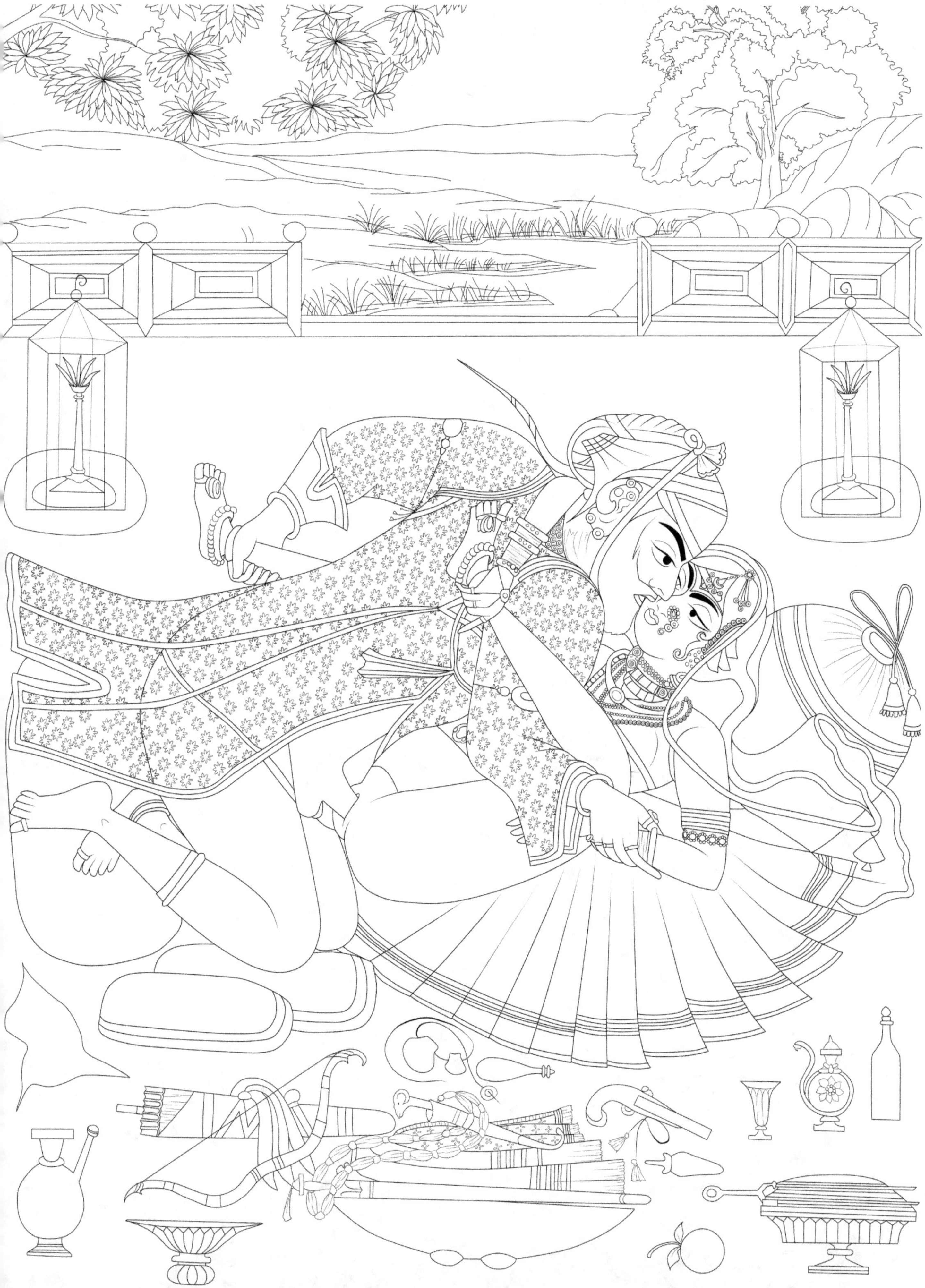

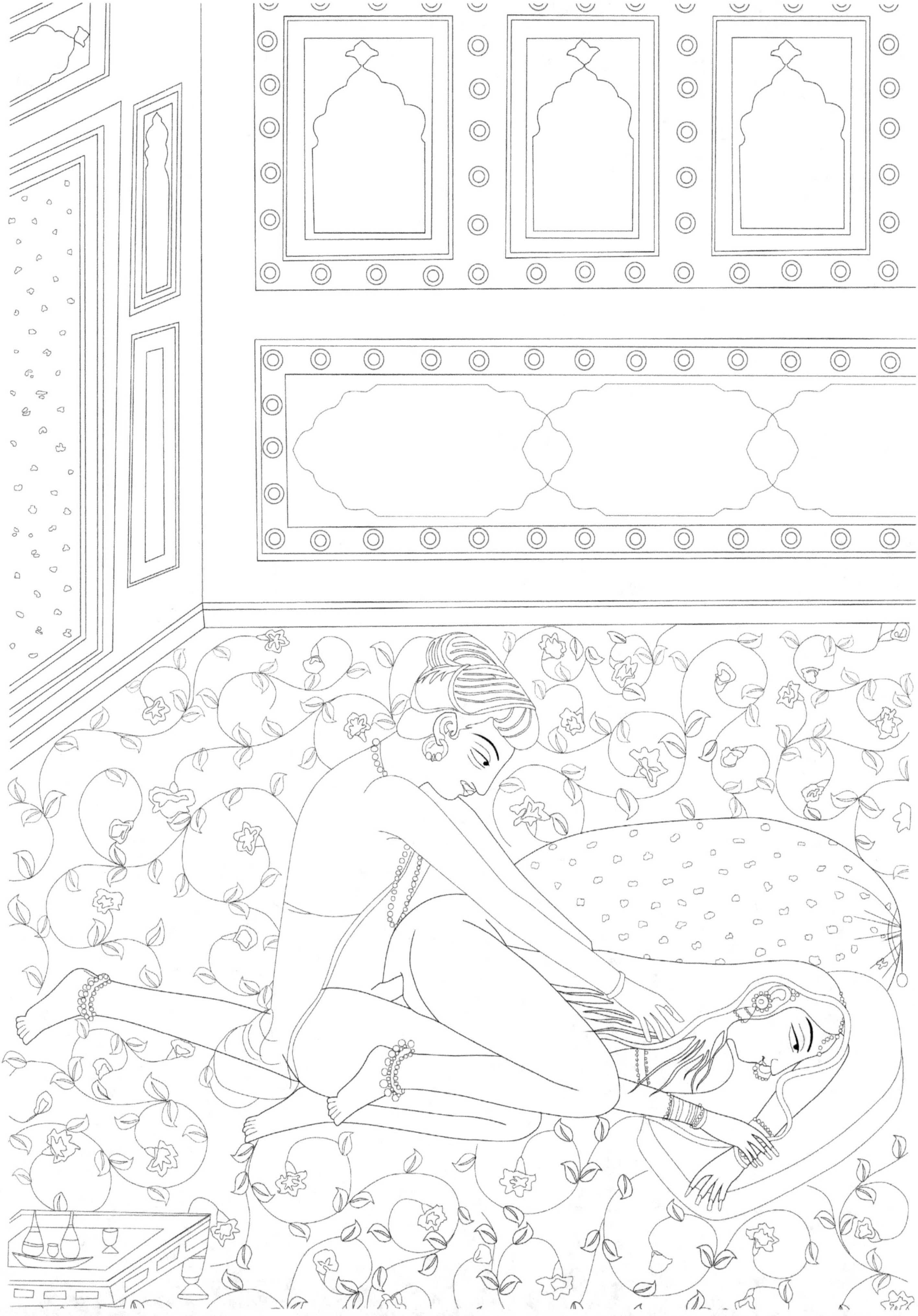

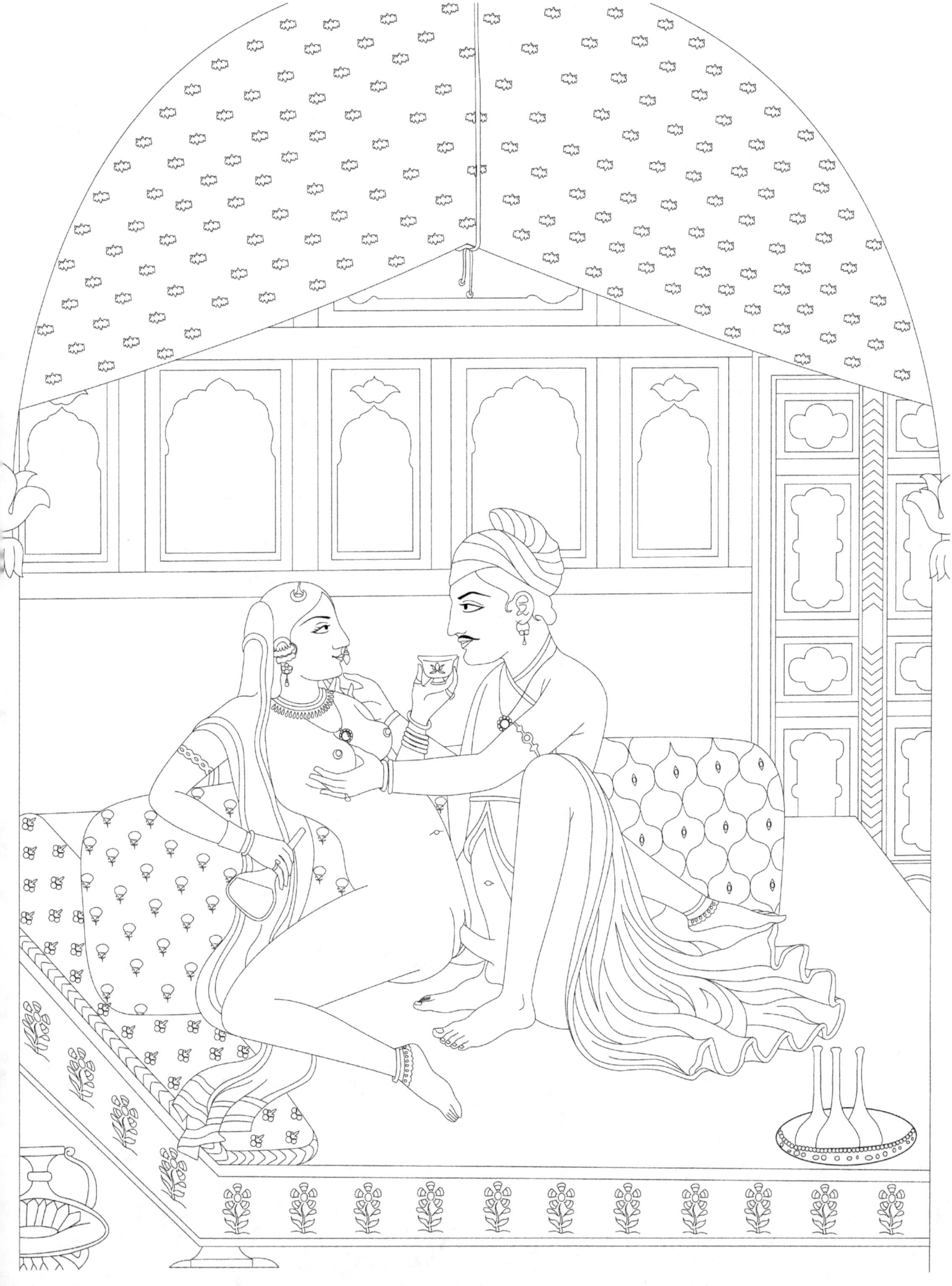

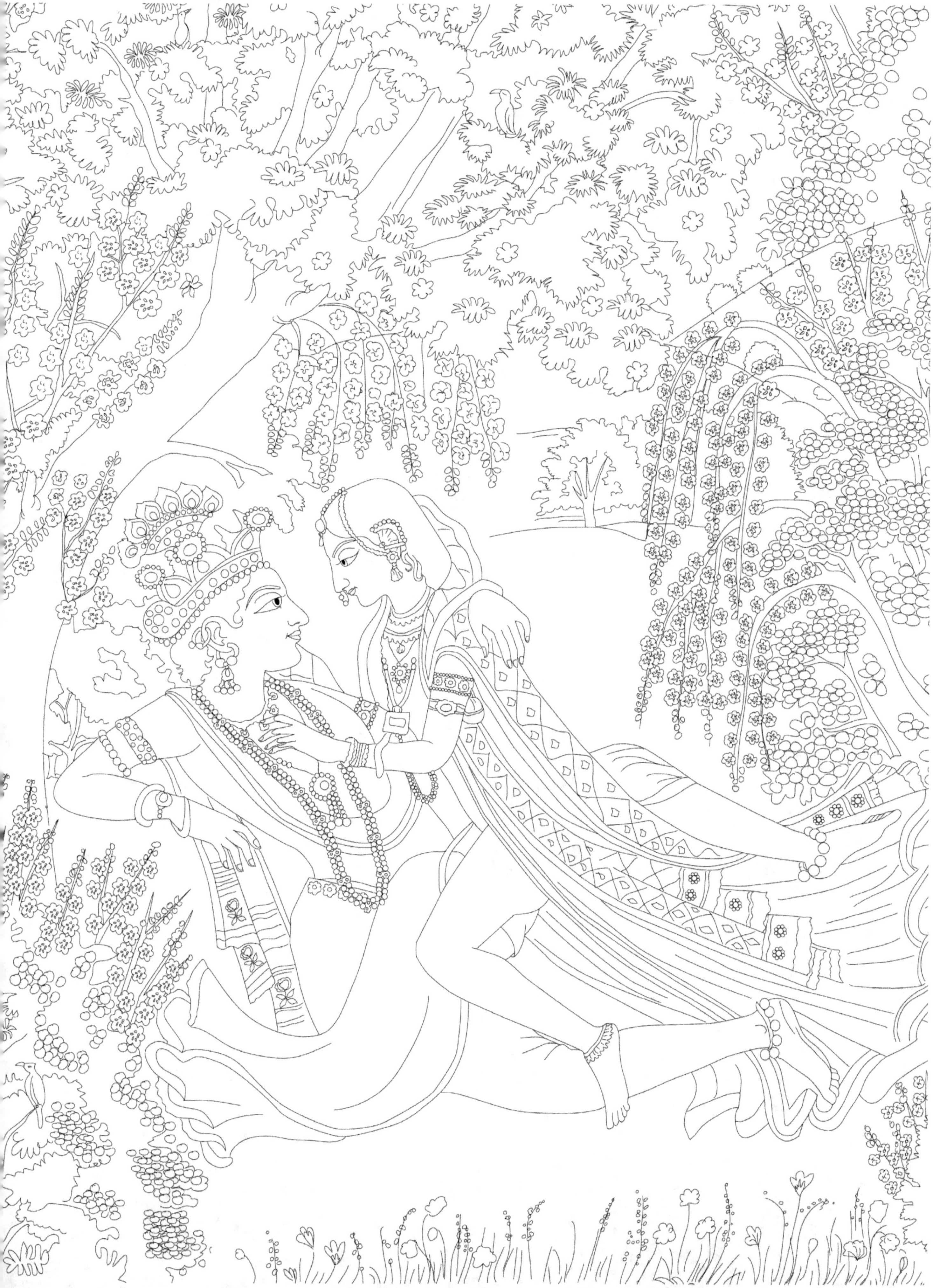

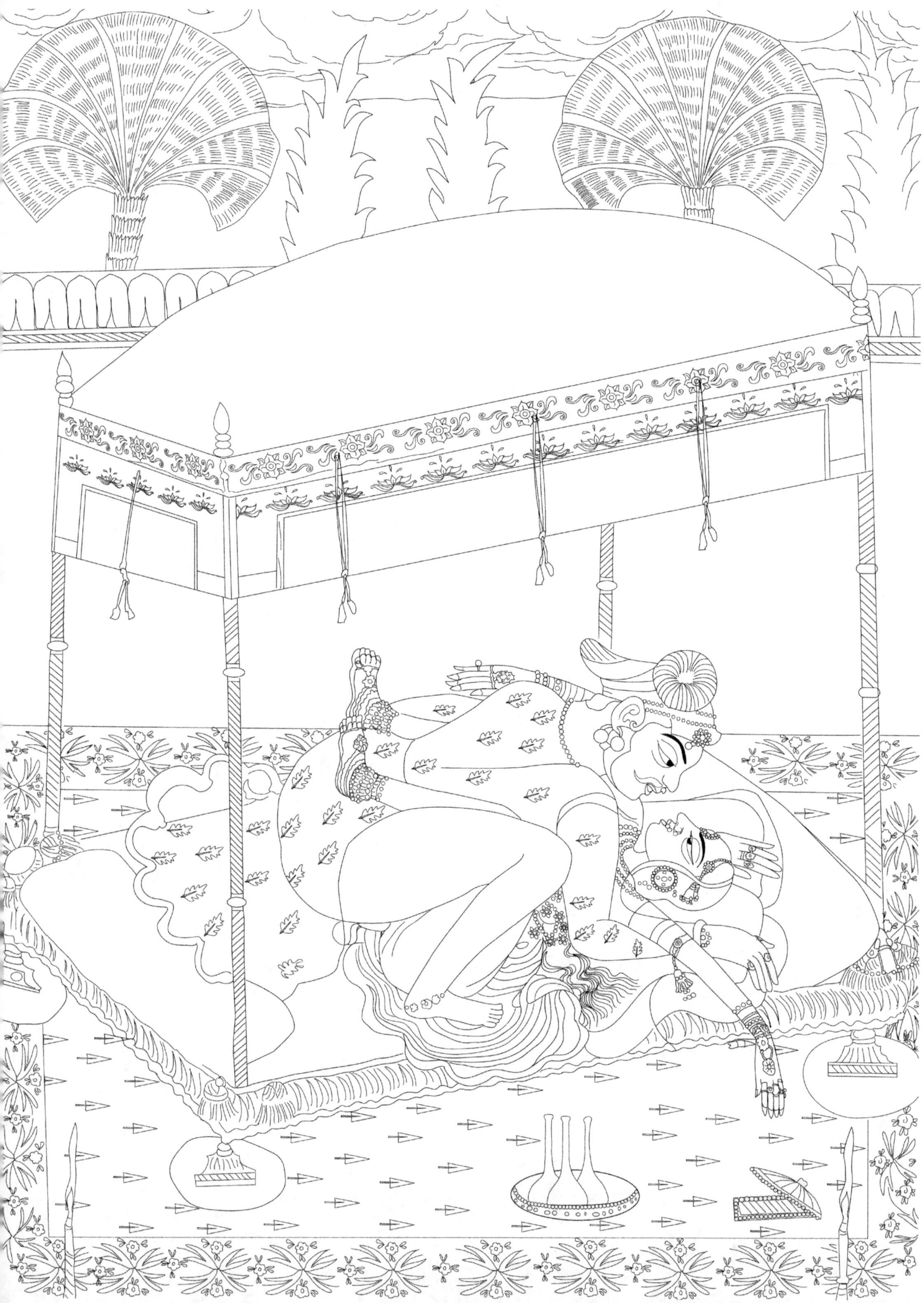

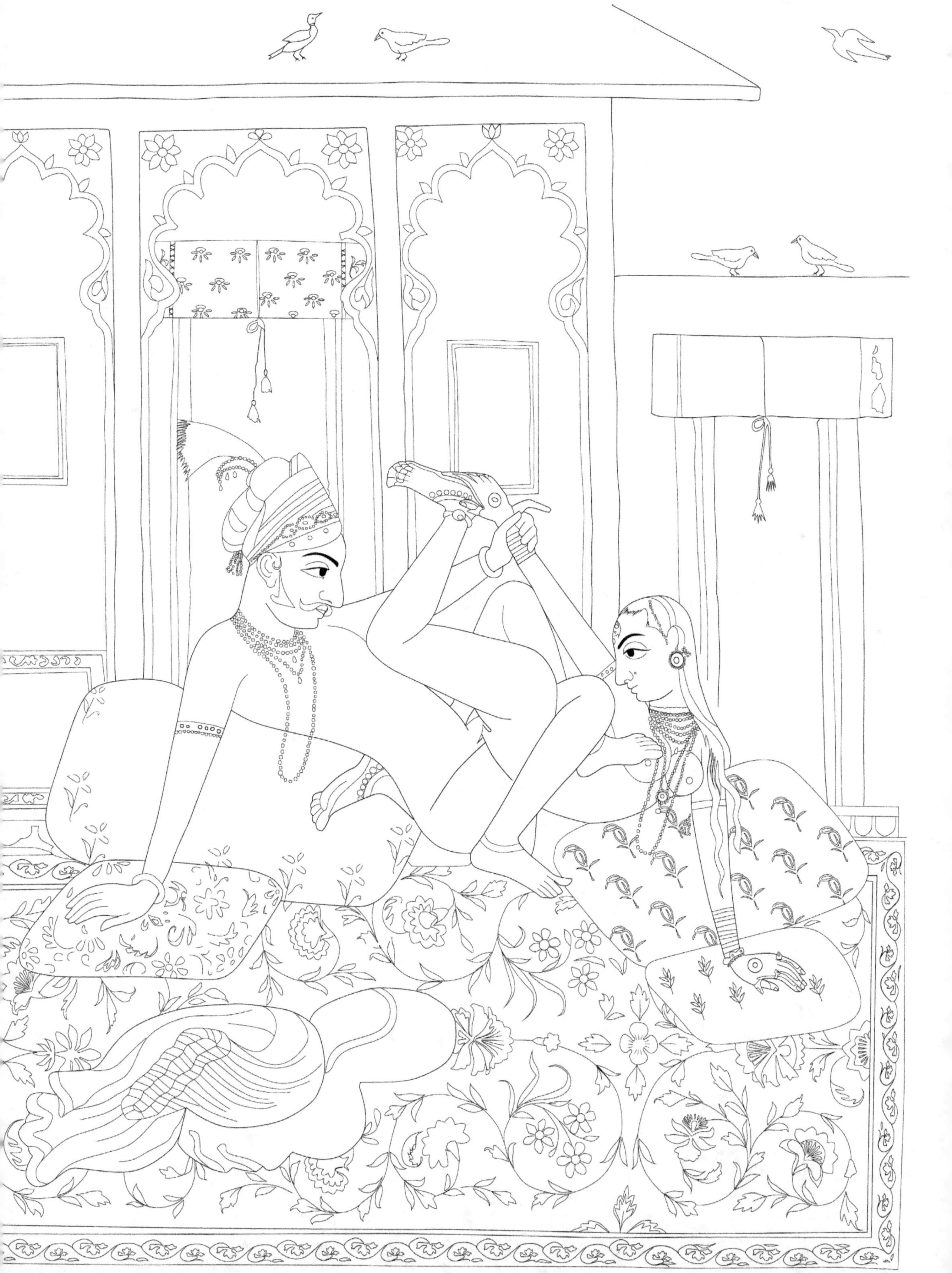

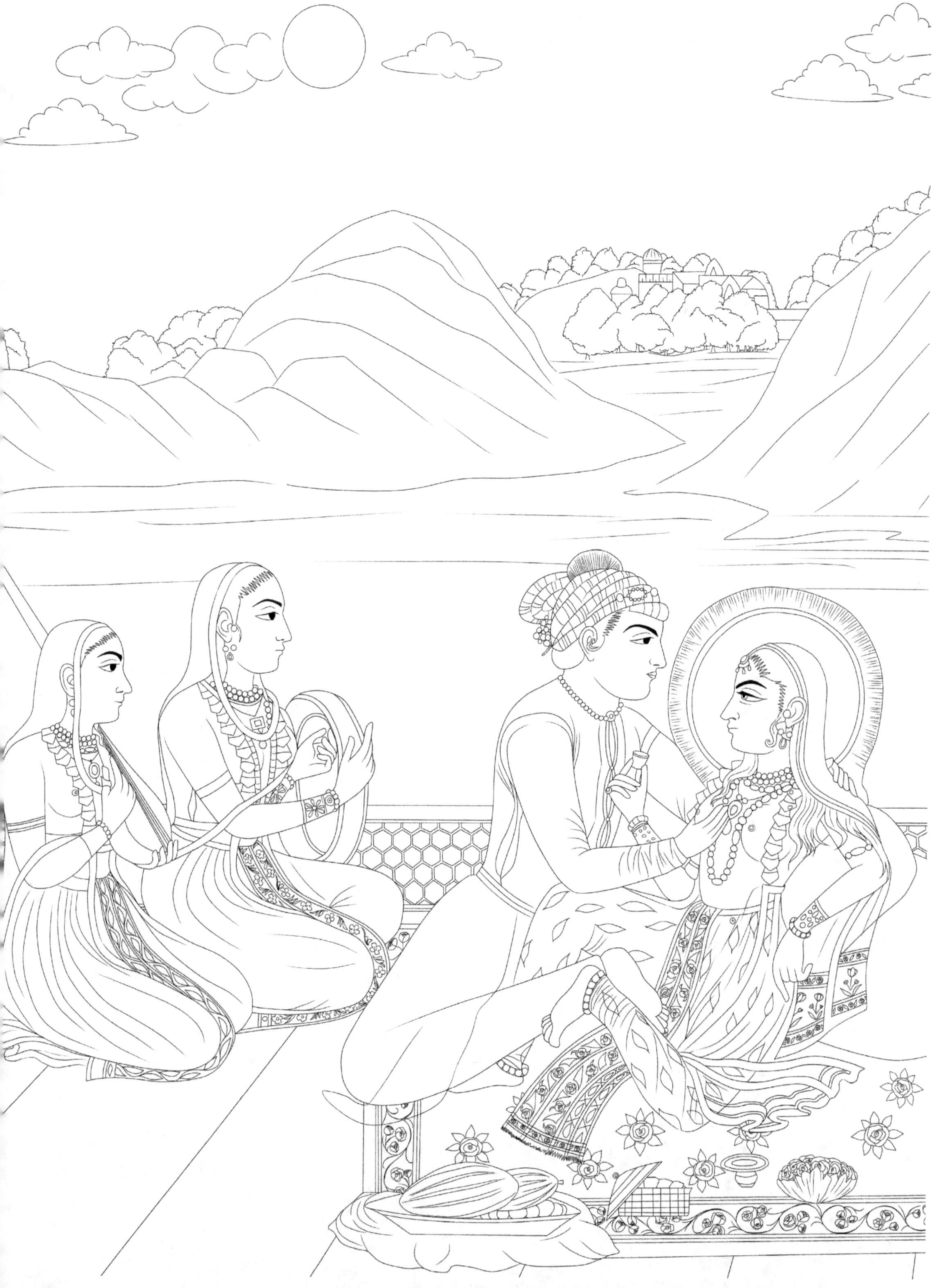

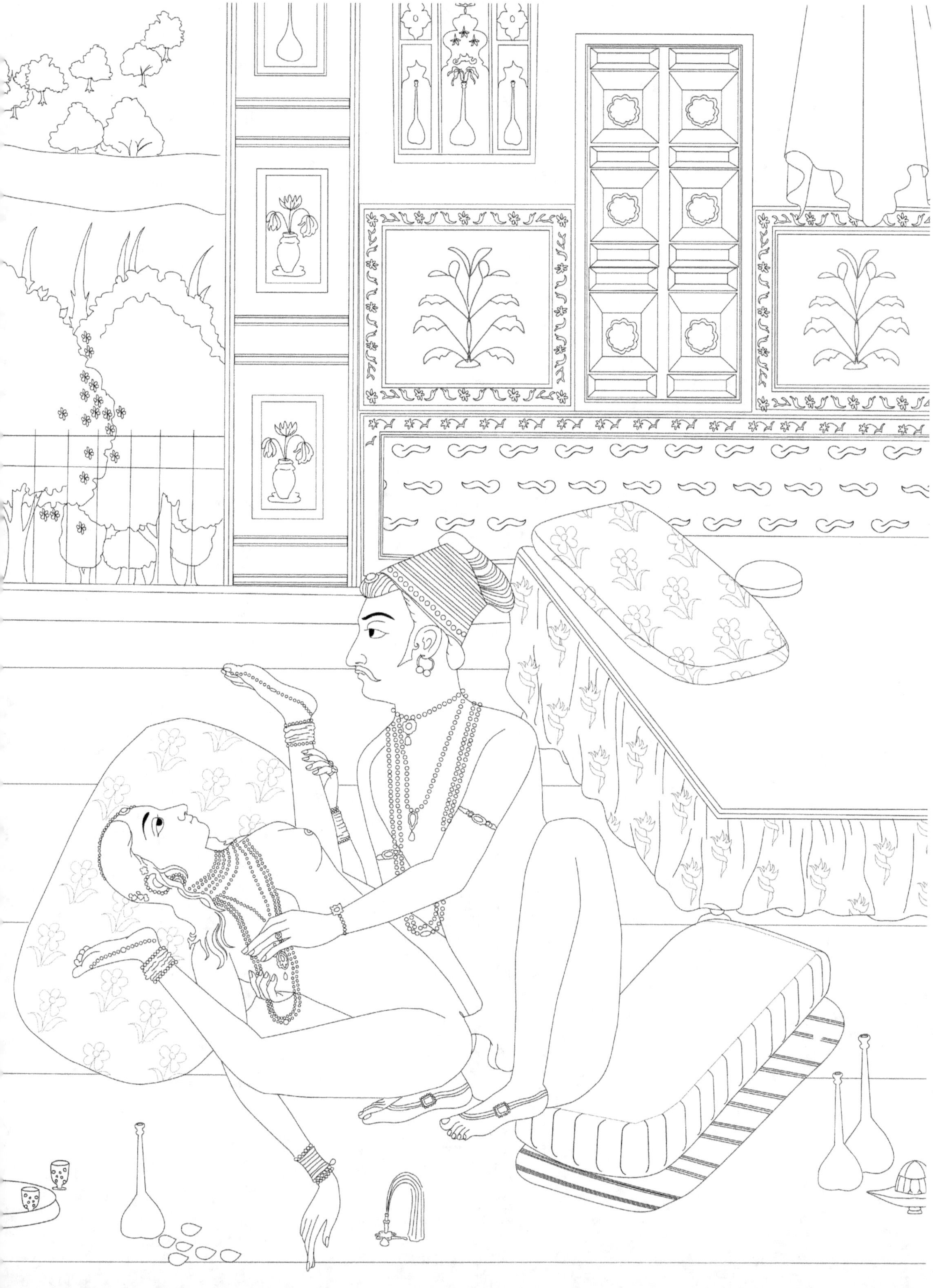

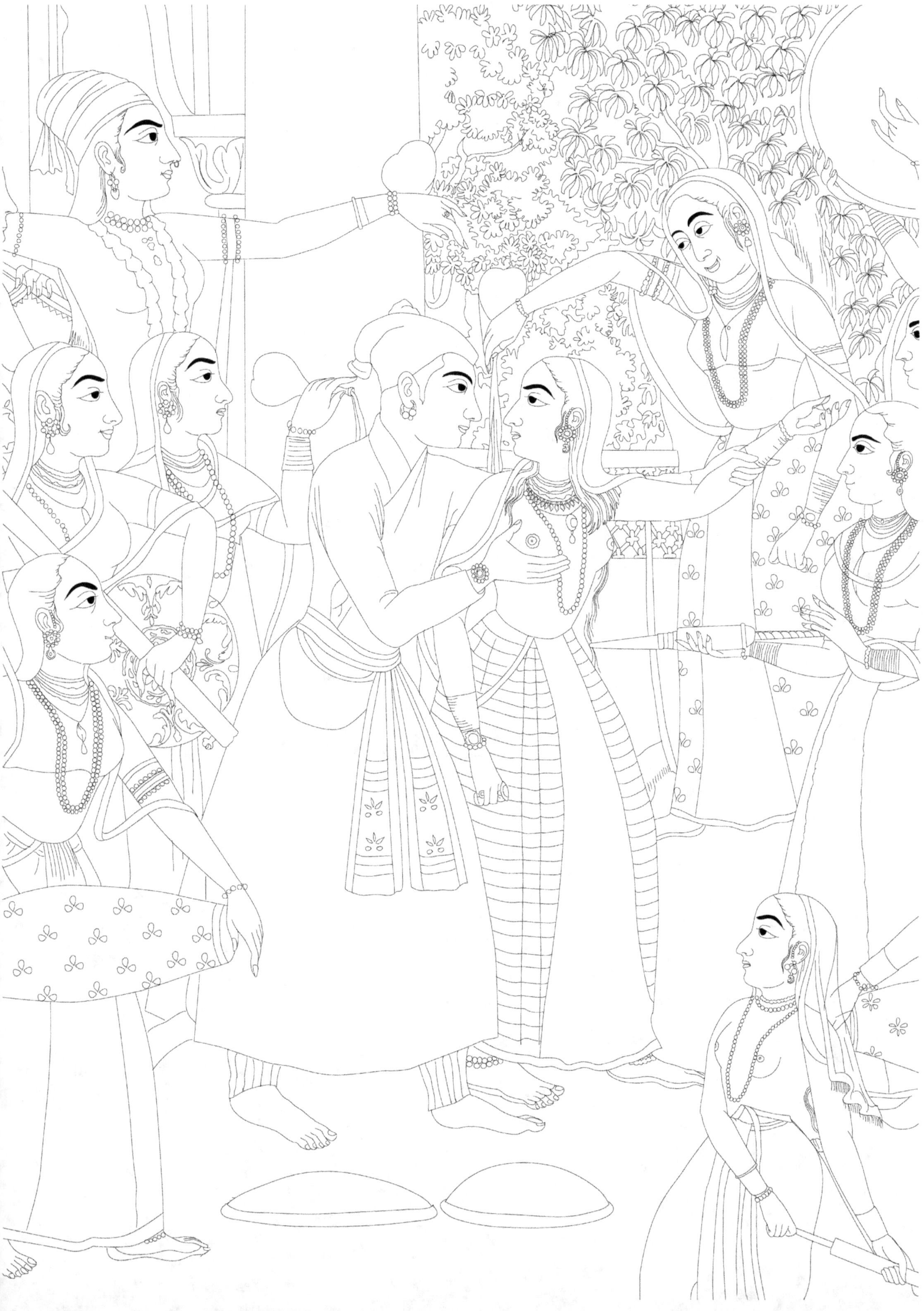

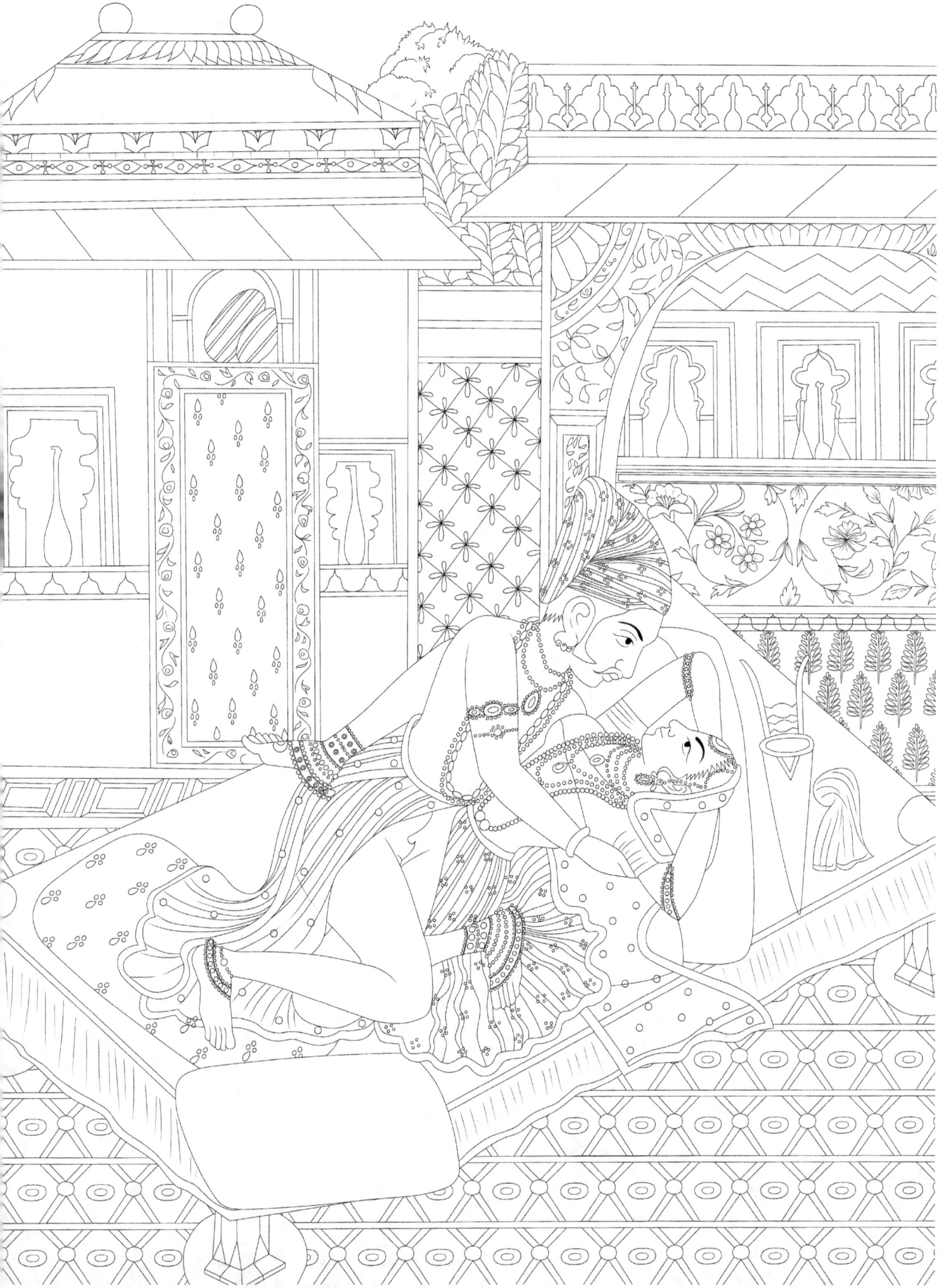

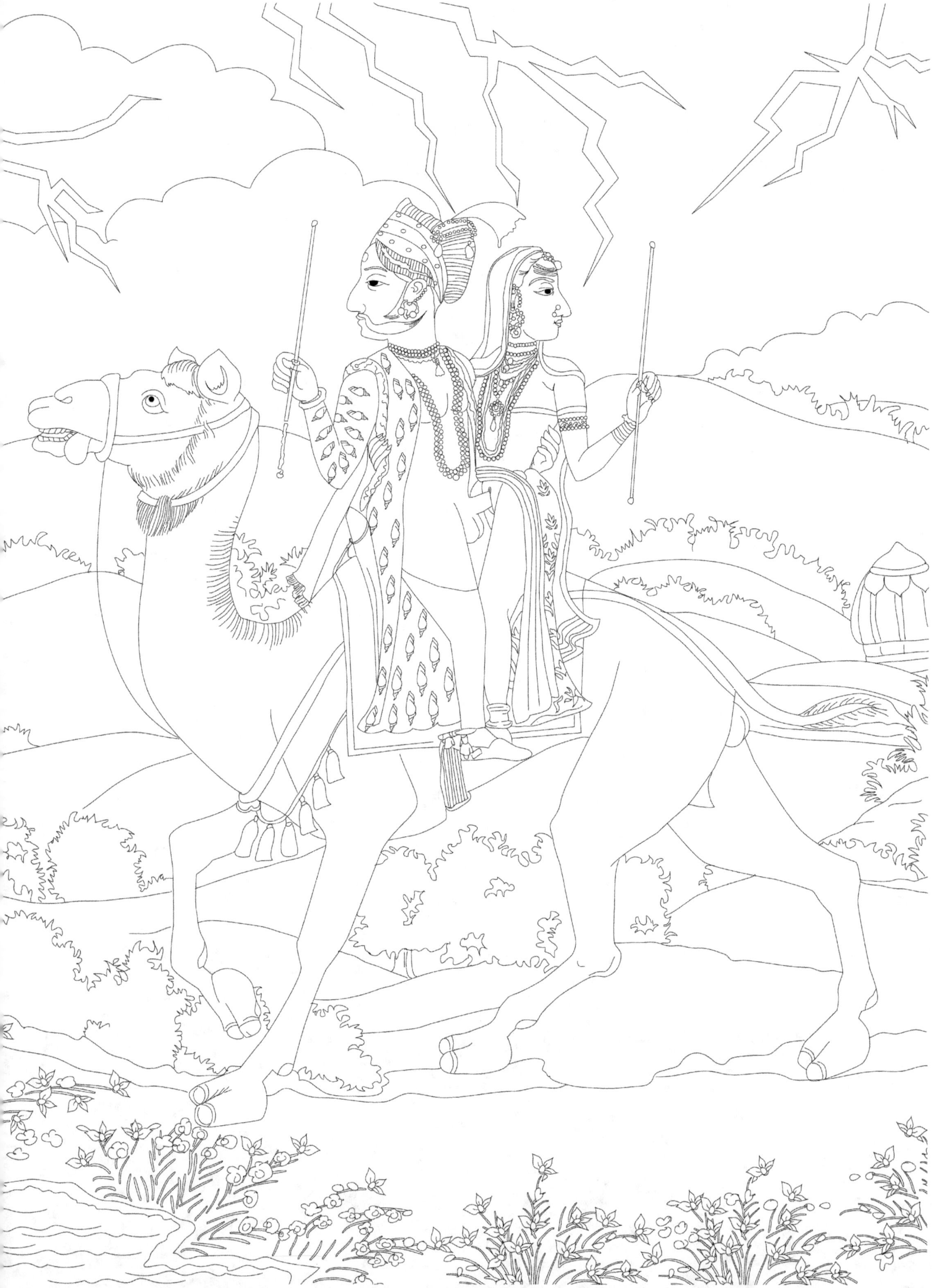

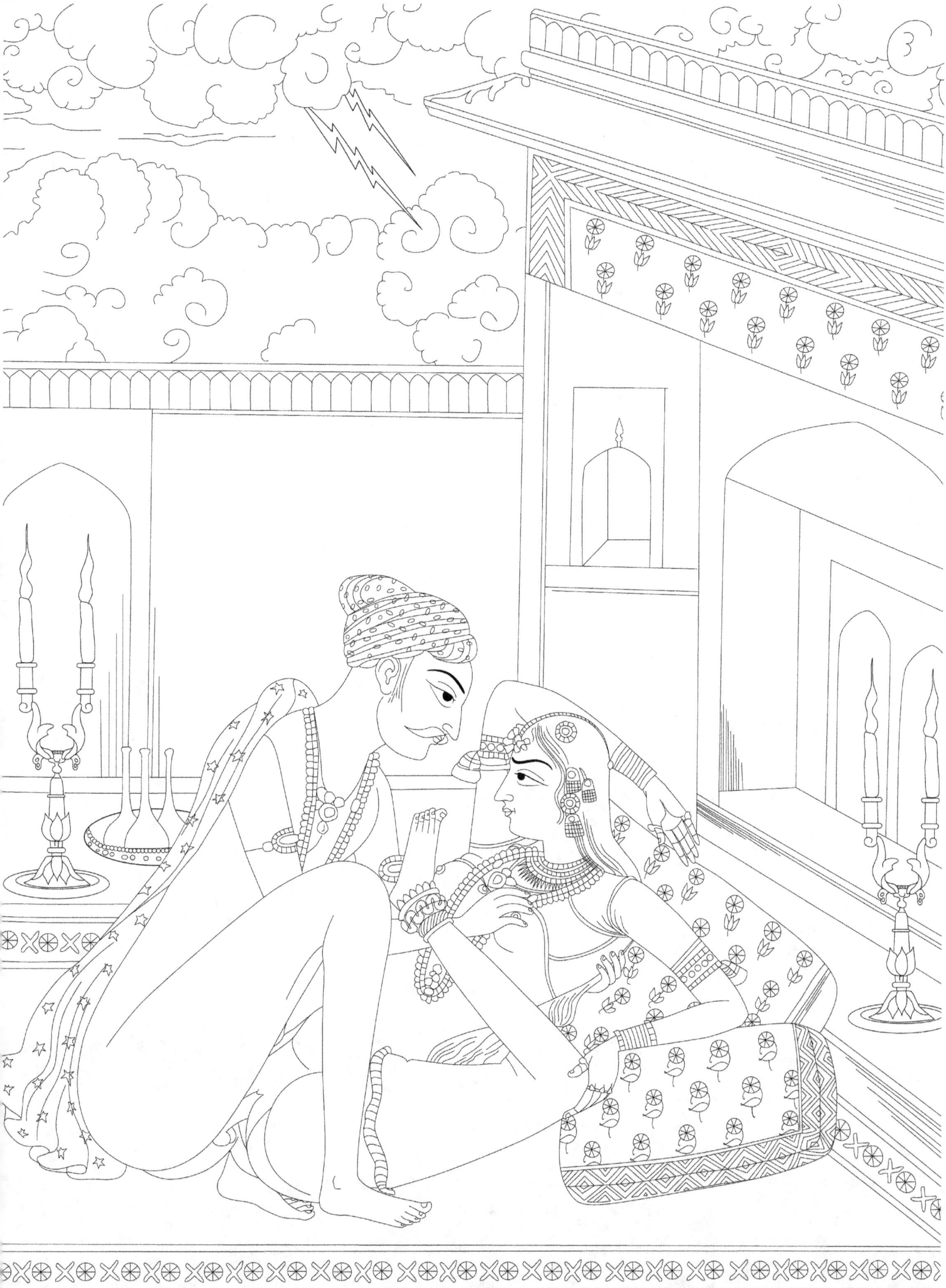

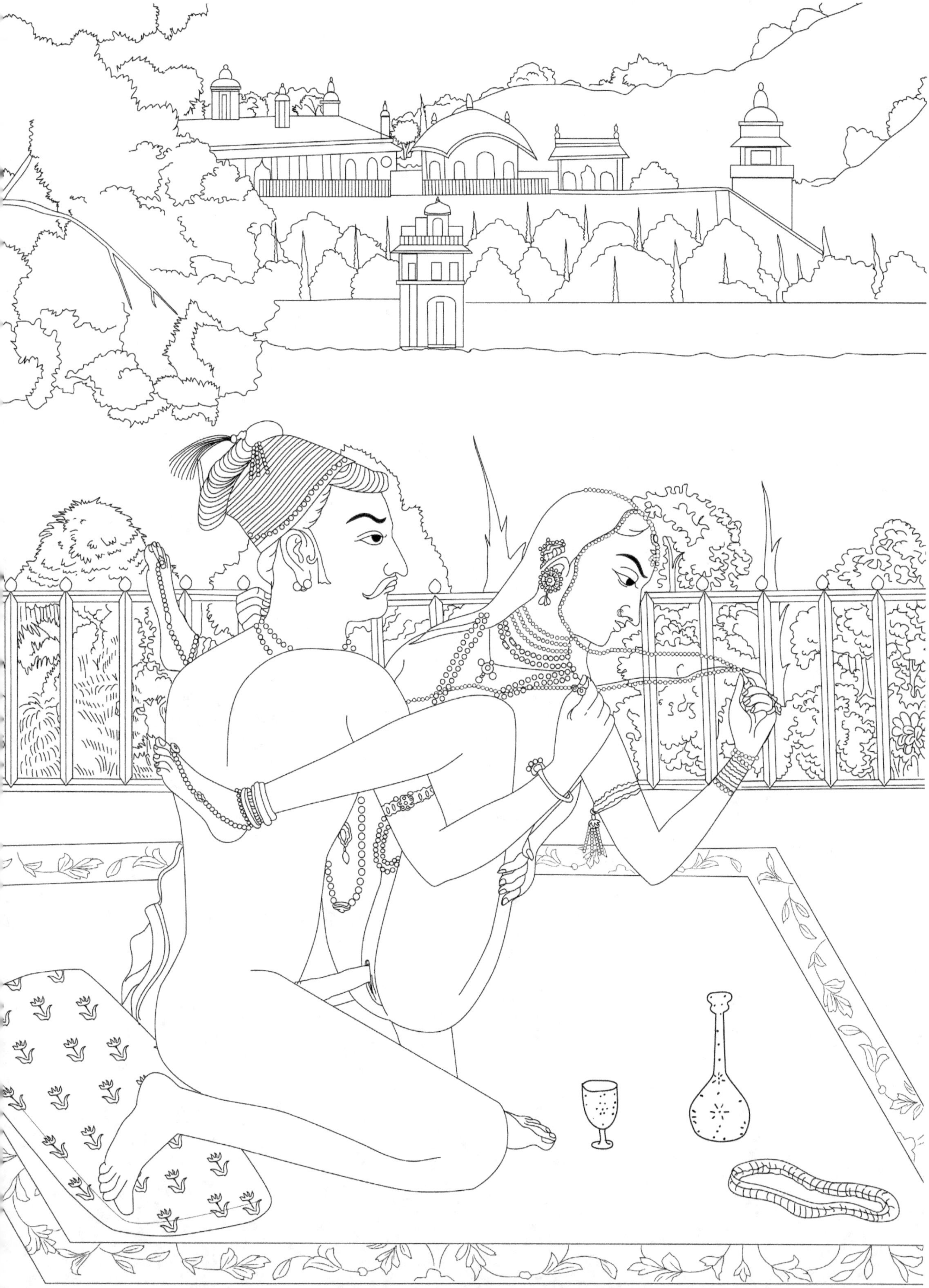

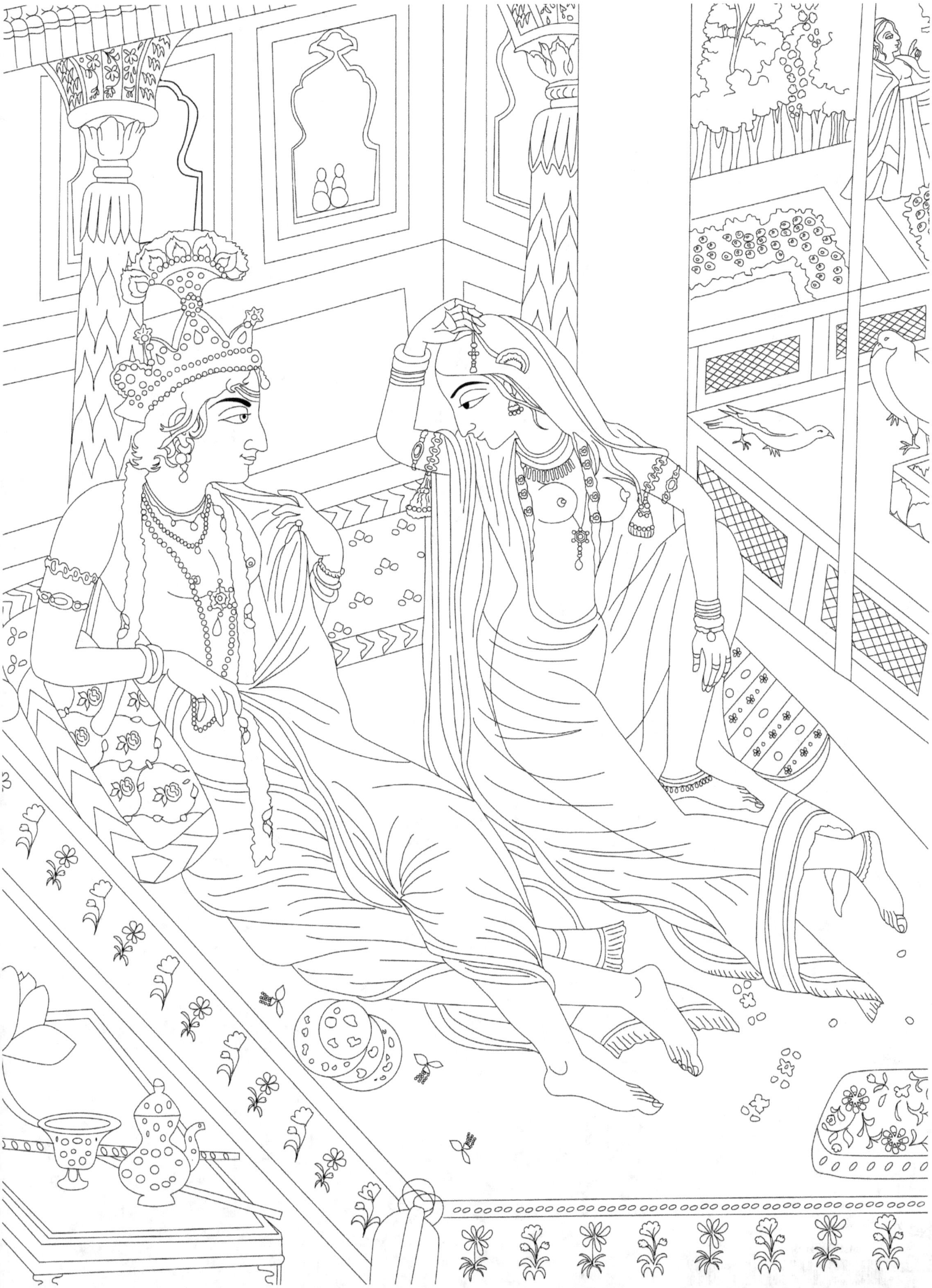

www.ingramcontent.com/pod-product-compliance
Lightning Source LLC
Chambersburg PA
CBHW081621220526
45468CB00010B/2982